EXTRATERRESTRIAL CIVILIZATIONS

Books on Astronomy by Isaac Asimov

The Clock We Live On
The Kingdom of the Sun
The Double Planet
Environments Out There
The Universe
To the Ends of the Universe
Jupiter, the Largest Planet
Asimov on Astronomy
Our World in Space
Eyes on the Universe
Alpha Centauri, the Nearest Star
The Collapsing Universe
Mars, the Red Planet
Saturn and Beyond

For Young Readers

The Moon
Mars
Stars
Galaxies
Comets and Meteors
The Sun
ABC's of Space
What Makes the Sun Shine?
The Solar System
How Did We Find Out About Comets?
How Did We Find Out About Outer Space?
How Did We Find Out About Black Holes?

the most magnificent redwood, the sweetest-smelling rose, the most ferocious Venus's-flytrap.*

When it comes to animals, however, matters are different. Animals move as we do and have recognizable needs and fears as we do. They eat, sleep, eliminate, reproduce, seek comfort, and avoid danger. Because of this, there is a tendency to read into their actions human motivation and human intelligence.

Thus, to the human imagination, ants and bees, which follow behavior that is purely instinctive and with little or no scope for individual variation, or for behavior change to meet unlooked-for eventualities, are viewed as being purposefully industrious.

The snake, which slithers through the grass because that is the only way its evolved shape and structure makes it possible for it to move, and which thus avoids notice and can strike before being seen, is imagined to be sly and subtle. (This characterization can be upheld on the authority of the Bible—see Genesis 3:1.)

In similar fashion, the donkey is thought of as stupid, the lion and eagle as proud and regal, the peacock as vain, the fox as cunning, and so on.

It is almost inevitable that wholesale attribution of human motivations to animal actions will lead one to take it for granted that if one could but establish communication with particular animals one would find them of human intelligence.

This is not to say that particular human beings, if pinned to the wall, will admit believing this. Nevertheless, we can watch Disney cartoons featuring animals with human intelligence and remain comfortably unaware of the incongruence.

Of course, such cartoons are just an amusing game, and the willing suspension of disbelief is a well-known characteristic of human beings. Then, too, Aesop's fables and the medieval chronicles of Reynard the Fox are not really about talking animals, but are ways of expressing truths about social abuses without risking the displeasure of those in power—who may not be bright enough to recognize that they are being satirized.

Nevertheless, the enduring popularity of these animal stories, to

* There are books that have been written describing how plants seem aware of human speech and react with apparent intelligence to it. As far as biologists can tell, however, there is no scientific merit whatever to such views.

which one can add Joel Chandler Harris's "Uncle Remus" tales and Hugh Lofting's "Dr. Dolittle" stories, shows a certain readiness in the human being to suspend disbelief in that particular direction; more so, perhaps, than in others. There is a sneaking feeling, I suspect, that if animals aren't as intelligent as we are, they ought to be.

We cannot even seek refuge in the fact that talking-animal stories are essentially for children. The recent best-sellerdom of *Watership Down* by Richard Adams is an example of a talking-animal book for adults that I found profoundly moving.

—And yet, side by side with this ancient and primordial feeling of cousinship with animals (even while we hunted them down or enslaved them) there is, in Western thought at least, the consciousness of an impassable gulf between human beings and other animals.

In the Biblical account of creation, the human being is created by God through an act different from that which created the rest of the animals. The human being is described as created in God's image and as being given dominion over the rest of creation.

This difference can be interpreted as meaning that the human being has a soul and that other animals do not; that there is a spark of divinity and immortality in human beings that is not present in other animals; that there is in human beings something that will survive death, while nothing of the sort is present in other animals.

All this falls outside the purview of science and can be disregarded. The influence of such religious views, however, makes it easier to believe that human beings alone are reasoning entities and that no other animal is. This, at least, is something that can be tested and observed by the usual methods of science.

Nevertheless, human beings have not been secure enough in the uniqueness of our species to be willing to let it stand the test of scientific investigation. There has even been a certain nervousness about the tendency of those biologists with a strong concept of order to classify living things into species, genera, orders, families, and so on.

By grouping animals according to greater and lesser resemblances, one develops a kind of tree of life with different species occupying different twigs of different branches. What starts out as an inescapable metaphor suggests only too clearly the possibility that the tree grew; that the branches developed.

In short, the mere classification of species leads inexorably to the

To put it most briefly, human beings, because they live in air, can develop hands with which they can manipulate their environment. Dolphins, because they live in water, cannot develop hands.

Then again, the fire that early humans learned to handle is the radiation of heat and light that results from a rapid energy-yielding chemical reaction. The most common energy-yielding large-scale chemical reactions that are useful in this connection are those resulting from the combination of substances containing carbon atoms, hydrogen atoms, or both ("fuel") with the oxygen in the air. The process is called combustion. Fire cannot exist under water since free oxygen is not present and combustion cannot take place.

Therefore, even if dolphins had the intelligence to conceptualize fire, and to work out, mentally, the steps needed to tame and use it, they would be unable to put any of it into practice.

We see now, however, that the human use of fire could be considered as no more than the accidental by-product of the fact that the human being lives in air, and is not in itself necessarily a true measure of intelligence.

The dolphins, after all, even though they are unable to manipulate the environment and unable to build and use a fire, may have in their own way developed a subtle philosophy of life. They may have worked out, more usefully than we have, a rationalization of living. They may interchange more joy and good will with their feelings and understand more. The fact that we cannot grasp their philosophy and their modes of thought is no evidence of their low intelligence, but is perhaps evidence of our own.

Well, *perhaps!*

The fact is, though, that we don't have any evidence of the dolphin's philosophy of life. The lack of that evidence may be entirely our fault, but there's nothing we can do about it. Without evidence, there is no way of reasoning usefully. We can look for the evidence and someday, perhaps, find it, but until then, we can't reasonably assign human intelligence to the dolphin.

Besides, even if our definition of human intelligence on the basis of fire is unfair and self-serving on some abstract scale, it will prove useful and reasonable for the purposes of this book. Fire sets us on a road that ends with a search for extraterrestrial intelligence; without fire we would never have made it.

The extraterrestrial intelligences we are looking for, then, must have developed the use of fire (or, to be fair, its equivalent) at some time in their history, or, as we are about to see, they could not have developed those attributes that would make it possible for them to be detected.

CIVILIZATION

Throughout the history of life, species of living creatures have made use of chemical energy by the slow combination of certain chemicals with oxygen within their cells. The process is analogous to combustion, but is slower and much more delicately controlled. Sometimes use is made of energy available in the bodies of stronger species as when a remora hitches a ride on a shark, or a human being hitches an ox to a plow.

Inanimate sources of energy are sometimes used when species allow themselves to be carried or moved by wind or by water currents. In those cases, though, the inanimate source of energy must be accepted at the place and time that it happens to be and in the amount that happens to exist.

The human use of fire involved an inanimate source of energy that was portable and could be used wherever desired. It could be ignited or extinguished at will and could be used when desired. It could be kept small or fed till it was large, and could be used in the quantities desired.

The use of fire made it possible for human beings, evolutionarily equipped for mild weather only, to penetrate the temperate zones. It made it possible for them to survive cold nights and long winters, to achieve security against fire-avoiding predators, and to roast meat and grain, thus broadening their diet and limiting the danger of bacterial and parasitic infestation.

Human beings multiplied in number and that meant there were more brains to plan future advances. With fire, life was not quite so hand-to-mouth, and there was more time to put those brains to work on something other than immediate emergencies.

In short, the use of fire put into motion an accelerating series of technological advances.

About 10,000 years ago, in the Middle East, a series of crucial advances were made. These included the development of agriculture,

CHAPTER 3

The Inner Solar System

NEARBY WORLDS

Once Galileo began to study the sky with his telescope, he could see that the various planets expanded into tiny orbs. They appeared as mere dots of light to the unaided eye merely because of their great distance.

What's more, Venus, being closer to the Sun than Earth is, showed phases like the Moon, as it should under such conditions if it were a dark body shining only by reflection. That was proof enough that the planets were also worlds, possibly more or less Earthlike.

Once that was established, it was taken for granted that all of them were life bearing and inhabited by intelligent creatures. Flammarion maintained this confidently, as I said in the previous chapter, as late as 1862.

The kinetic theory of gases, however, ruled out not merely the Moon as an abode of life, but any world smaller than itself. Any worlds smaller than the Moon could scarcely be expected to possess air or water. They would lack the gravitational field for it. Consider the asteroids, the first of which was discovered in 1801. They circle

41

the Sun just outside the orbit of Mars and the largest of them is but 1,000 kilometers (620 miles) in diameter. There are anywhere from 40,000 to 100,000 of them with diameters of at least a kilometer or 2, and every last one of them lacks air or liquid water* and are therefore without life.

The same is true for the two tiny satellites of Mars, discovered in 1877. They are in all likelihood captured asteroids, and have neither air nor liquid water.

Within the orbits of the asteroids lies the "inner Solar system" and there we find four planetary bodies larger than the Moon. In addition to the Earth itself, we have Mercury, Venus, and Mars.

Of these, Mercury is the smallest, but it is 4.4 times as massive as the Moon and its diameter is 4,860 kilometers (3,020 miles), which is 1.4 times that of the Moon. Mercury's surface gravity is 2.3 times that of the Moon and nearly 2/5 that of the Earth. Might it not manage to retain a thin atmosphere?

Not so. Mercury is also the closest of the planets to the Sun. At its nearest approach to the Sun it is at only 3/10 the distance from it that the Earth is. Any air it might have would be heated to far higher temperatures than the Earth's atmosphere. Gas molecules on Mercury would be correspondingly speedier in their motion and harder to hold onto. Mercury, therefore, would be expected to be as airless and waterless—and as lifeless—as the Moon.

In 1974 and 1975, a rocket probe, *Mariner 10,* passed near Mercury's surface on three occasions. On the third occasion, it passed within 327 kilometers (203 miles) of the surface. Mercury was mapped in detail and its surface was found to be cratered in a very Moonlike way, and its airlessness and waterlessness is confirmed. There is no perceptible doubt as to its lifelessness.

Venus looks far more hopeful. Venus's diameter is 12,100 kilometers (7,520 miles) as compared with Earth's 12,740 kilometers (7,920 miles). Venus's mass is about 0.815 times that of the Earth and its surface gravity is 0.90 times that of the Earth.

Even allowing for the fact that Venus is closer to the Sun than

---

* There may be small amounts of water in the solid state (ice) held to the asteroids and other small worlds by chemical bonds that don't depend on gravitational forces for their efficacy. Frozen water, however, is not suitable for life and even on Earth the frozen ice sheets of Greenland and Antarctica are life free in their natural state.

Earth and would therefore be hotter than Earth, it would seem that Venus should have an atmosphere. Its gravitational field is strong enough for that.

And, indeed, Venus *does* have an atmosphere, a very pronounced one, and one that is far cloudier than ours. Venus is wrapped in a planet-girdling perpetual cloud cover, which was at once taken as adequate evidence that there was water on Venus.

The cloud cover does, unfortunately, detract from the hopeful views we can have of Venus, since it prevents us from gathering evidence as to its fitness for life. At no time could astronomers ever catch a glimpse of its surface, however good their telescopes. They could not tell how rapidly Venus might rotate on its axis, how tipped that axis might be, how extensive its oceans (if any) might be, or anything else about it. Without more evidence than the mere existence of an atmosphere and clouds it was difficult to come to reasonable conclusions about life on Venus.

Mars's, on the other hand, is at once less hopeful and more hopeful.

It is less hopeful because it is distinctly smaller than Earth. Its diameter is only 6,790 kilometers (4,220 miles) and its mass is only 0.107 that of the Earth. With a mass only 1/10 that of Earth it is not exactly a large world, but on the other hand it is 8.6 times as massive as the Moon, so it is not exactly a small one, either. It is, in fact, twice as massive as Mercury.

Mars's surface gravity is 2.27 times that of the Moon and is just about that of Mercury. Mars, however, is four times as far from the Sun as Mercury is, so that Mars is considerably the cooler of the two. Mars's gravitational field need deal with considerably slower molecules for that reason.

It follows that although Mercury is without an atmosphere, Mars may have one—and it does. Mars's atmosphere is a thin one, to be sure, but it is distinctly there. Mars is presumably drier than the Earth, for its atmosphere is not as cloudy as Earth's (let alone Venus's), but occasional clouds are seen. Dust storms are also seen, so there must be sharp winds on Mars.

The more hopeful aspect of Mars is that its atmosphere is sufficiently thin and cloud free to allow its surface to be seen (rather vaguely) from Earth. For centuries, astronomers have done their best to map what it was they saw on that distant world. (At its closest, Mars can approach as closely as 56,000,000 kilometers [34,800,000 miles] to Earth, a distance that is 146 times as far away from us as the Moon.)

The first to make out a marking that others could see as well was the Dutch astronomer Christiaan Huygens (1629–1695). In 1659, he followed the markings he could see as they moved around the planet and determined the rotation period of Mars to be only a trifle longer than that of Earth. We now know Mars rotates in 24.66 hours compared to Earth's 24.

In 1781, the German-English astronomer William Herschel (1738–1822) * noted that Mars's axis of rotation was tilted to the perpendicular, as Earth's was, and almost by the same amount. Mars's axial tilt is 25.17° as compared with Earth's 23.45°.

This means that not only does Mars have a day-night alteration much as Earth has, but also seasons. Of course, Mars is half again as far from the Sun as we are, so that its seasons are colder than ours. Furthermore, it takes Mars longer to complete its orbit about the Sun, 687 days to our 365¼, so that the seasons on Mars are each nearly twice as long as ours.

In 1784, Herschel noted that there were ice caps about the Martian poles, as there were about Earth's poles. There was one more point of resemblance in that the ice caps were assumed to be frozen water, and therefore to serve as proof there was water on Mars.

Mars and Venus both looked like hopeful possible abodes of life, certainly far more hopeful than the asteroids or the Moon or Mercury.

VENUS

In 1796, the French astronomer Pierre Simon de Laplace (1749–1827) speculated on the origin of the Solar system.

The Sun rotates on its axis in a counterclockwise direction when viewed from a point far above its north pole. From that same point,

---

* He was the father of John Herschel, who a half-century later was to be victimized by the Moon Hoax.

all the planets known to Laplace moved about the Sun in a counterclockwise direction, and all the planets whose rotations were known rotated about their axes in a counterclockwise direction. Added to that was the fact that all the satellites known to Laplace revolved about their planets in a counterclockwise direction.

Finally, all the planets had orbits that were nearly in the plane of the Sun's equator and all the satellites had orbits that were nearly in the plane of their planet's equator.

To account for all this, Laplace suggested that the Solar system was originally a vast cloud of dust and gas called a nebula (from the Latin word for *cloud*). The nebula was turning slowly in a counterclockwise direction. Its own gravitational field slowly contracted it, and as it contracted it had to spin faster and faster in accordance with something called the law of conservation of angular momentum. Eventually, it condensed to form the Sun, which is still spinning in the counterclockwise direction.

As the cloud contracted on its way to the Sun and as it increased its rate of spin, the centrifugal effect of rotation caused it to belly out at its equator. (This happens to the Earth, which has an equatorial bulge that lifts points on its equator 13 miles farther from the center of the Earth than the north and south poles are.)

The bulge of the contracting nebula became more and more pronounced as it shrank further and speeded up further, until the entire bulge was thrown off like a thin doughnut around the contracting nebula. As the nebula continued to shrink, additional doughnuts of matter were shed.

Each doughnut, in Laplace's view, gradually condensed into a planet, maintaining the original counterclockwise spin, and speeding up that spin as it condensed. As each planet formed there was a chance it might shed smaller subsidiary doughnuts of its own, which became the satellites. The rings around Saturn are examples of matter that has been given off (according to Laplace's nebular hypothesis) and has not yet condensed to a satellite.

The nebular hypothesis explains why all the revolutions and rotations in the Solar system should be in the same direction.* It is because all participate in the spin of the original nebula.

* Today, we know of some exceptions.

It also explains why all the planets revolve in the plane of the Sun's equator. It is because it is from the Sun's equatorial regions that they were originally formed; and it is from the planetary equatorial regions that the satellites formed.

The nebular hypothesis was more or less accepted by astronomers during the nineteenth century, and it added detail to the picture that people drew of Mars and Venus.

As the nebula condensed, according to this theory, it would seem that the planets would form in order from the outermost to the innermost. In other words, after the nebula had condensed to the point where it was only 500,000,000 kilometers (310,000,000 miles) across, it gave off the ring of matter that formed Mars. Then, after considerable time taken up in further contraction, it gave off the matter that formed the Earth and the Moon, and after another unknown length of time, the matter that formed Venus.

By the nebular hypothesis, therefore, it would seem that Mars was considerably older than Earth, and that Earth was considerably older than Venus.

It became customary, therefore, to think of Mars as having moved farther along the evolutionary path than Earth; not only with respect to its planetary characteristics, but with respect to the life upon it. Similarly, Venus had not moved as far along the evolutionary path. Thus, the Swedish chemist Svante August Arrhenius (1859–1927) drew an eloquent picture in 1918 of Venus as a water-soaked jungle.

This sort of thinking was reflected in science fiction stories, which very often depicted Mars as occupied by an intelligent race with a long history that dwarfed that of Earthly human beings. The Martians were pictured as far advanced beyond us technologically, but often as decadent and weary of life—in their old age as a species.

On the other hand, many stories were written of a junglelike Venus, or one with a plantetary ocean—in either case filled with primitive life forms. In 1954, I myself published a novel, *Lucky Starr and the Oceans of Venus,* in which the planet was described as having a planetary ocean. But only two years later our thoughts about Venus were revolutionized.

After World War II, astronomers gained a large number of new and extraordinarily useful tools for the exploration of the worlds of

On November 28, 1964, the first successful Mars probe, *Mariner 4,* was launched. As *Mariner 4* passed Mars it took a series of twenty photographs that were turned into radio signals beamed back to Earth, where they were turned into photographs again.

What did they show? Canals? Any signs of a high civilization or, at least, of life?

What the photographs showed turned out to be completely unexpected, for as they were received, astronomers saw what were clearly craters—craters that looked very much like those on the Moon.

The craters, at least as they showed up on the *Mariner 4* pictures, seemed so many and so sharp that the natural conclusion was that there had been very little erosion. That seemed to mean not only thin air, but very little life activity. The craters shown in the photographs of *Mariner 4* seemed to be the mark of a dead world.

Mariner 4 was designed to pass behind Mars (as viewed from Earth) after its flyby, so that its radio signals would eventually pass through the Martian atmosphere on their way to Earth. From the changes in the signals, astronomers could deduce the density of the Martian atmosphere.

It turned out that the Martian atmosphere was even thinner than the lowest estimates. It was less than 1/100 as dense as Earth's atmosphere. The air pressure at the surface of Mars is about equal to that of Earth's atmosphere at a height of 32 kilometers (19 miles) above the Earth's surface. This was another blow to the possibility of advanced life on Mars.

In 1969, two more rocket probes, *Mariner 6* and *Mariner 7,* were sent past Mars. They had better cameras and instruments, and took more photographs. The new and much better photographs showed that there was no mistake about the craters. The Martian surface was riddled with them—as thickly, in places, as the Moon.

The new probes, however, showed that Mars was not entirely like the Moon. There were regions in the photographs in which the Martian surface seemed flat and featureless and others where the surface seemed jumbled and broken in a way that was not characteristic of either Moon or Earth. There were still no signs of canals.

On May 30, 1971, *Mariner 9* was launched and sent on its way to Mars. This probe was not merely going to pass by Mars, it was to go into orbit about it. On November 13, 1971, it went into orbit. Mars was at that time in the midst of a planet-wide dust storm and nothing could be seen, but *Mariner 9* waited. In December, 1971, the dust storm finally settled down and *Mariner 9* got to work taking photographs of Mars. The entire planet was mapped in detail.

The first thing that was settled, once and for all, was that there were no canals on Mars. Lowell was wrong after all. What he had seen was an optical illusion.

Nor were the dark areas either water or vegetation. Mars seemed all desert, but here and there one found dark streaks that usually started from some small crater or other elevation. They seemed to be composed of dust particles blown by the wind and tended to collect where an elevation broke the force of the wind, on the side of the elevation away from the wind.

There were occasional light streaks, too, the difference between the two resting perhaps in the size of the particles. The possibility that the dark and light areas were differences in dust markings and that the dark areas expanded in the spring because of seasonal wind changes had been suggested a few years earlier by the American astronomer Carl Sagan (1935–   ). *Mariner 9* proved him to be completely correct.

Only one of the hemispheres of Mars was cratered and Moon-like; the other was marked by giant volcanoes and giant canyons, and seemed geologically alive.

One feature of the Martian surface roused considerable curiosity. These were markings that wiggled their way across the Martian surface like rivers and that had branches that looked for all the world like tributaries. Then, too, both polar ice caps seemed to exist in layers. At the edge, where they are melting, they looked just like a slanted stack of thin poker chips.

It is possible to suppose that Mars's history is one of weather cycles. It may now be in a frigid cycle, with most of the water frozen in the ice caps and in the soil. In the past, and possibly again in the future, it may be in a mild cycle, in which the ice caps melt, releasing both water and carbon dioxide, so that the atmosphere becomes thicker and the rivers grow full.

In that case, even if there is no apparent life on Mars now there may have been in the past, and there may again be in the future. As for the present, life forms could be hibernating in the frozen soil, in the form of spores.

testing. Nevertheless, if life is present, there seems very little chance that it is anything more than very primitive in nature—no more than on the level of bacterial life on Earth.

Such simple life would be quite sufficient to excite biologists and astronomers, but as far as the search for extraterrestrial intelligence is concerned, we are left with what is overwhelmingly likely to be zero.

We must look elsewhere.

CHAPTER 4

The Outer Solar System

PLANETARY CHEMISTRY

The inner Solar system out to the orbit of Mars is a comparatively small structure. Beyond Mars is the "outer Solar system," which is far vaster and within which giant planets orbit. There are no less than four such giants out there: Jupiter, Saturn, Uranus, and Neptune. Each dwarfs Earth, particularly Jupiter, which has over 1,000 times the volume of Earth and over 300 times its mass.

Why should the inner Solar system contain pygmies and the outer Solar system giants? Consider—

The cloud out of which the Solar system was formed would naturally have been made up of the same kind of substances that make up the Universe generally—more or less. Astronomers have, through spectroscopy, determined the chemical structure of the Sun and of other stars, as well as of the dust and gas between the stars. They have therefore come to some conclusions as to the general elementary makeup of the Universe. This is given in the accompanying table:

Element	Number of Atoms for every 10,000,000 Atoms of Hydrogen
Hydrogen	10,000,000
Helium	1,400,000
Oxygen	6,800
Carbon	3,000
Neon	2,800
Nitrogen	910
Magnesium	290
Silicon	250
Sulfur	95
Iron	80
Argon	42
Aluminum	19
Sodium	17
Calcium	17
all other elements combined	50

As you see, the Universe is essentially hydrogen and helium, the two elements with the simplest atoms. Together hydrogen and helium make up nearly 99.9 percent of all the atoms in the Universe. Hydrogen and helium are, of course, very light atoms, not nearly as heavy as the others, but they still make up about 98 percent of all the mass in the Universe.

The fourteen most common elements given in the table above make up almost the entire Universe. Only one atom out of a quarter million is anything else.

Of the fourteen, the atoms of helium, neon, and argon do not combine either with each other or with the atoms of other elements.

Hydrogen atoms will combine with other atoms after colliding with them. In view of the makeup of the Universe, however, hydrogen atoms will, if they collide with anything at all, collide with other hydrogen atoms. The result is the formation of hydrogen molecules, made up of two hydrogen atoms each.

Oxygen, nitrogen, carbon, and sulfur are made up of atoms that are likely to combine with hydrogen atoms when the latter are present in overwhelming quantity. Each oxygen atom combines with two hydrogen atoms to form molecules of water. Each nitrogen atom

CHAPTER 5

The Stars

SUBSTARS

Having gone rather exhaustively through the Solar system, it would appear that although there may be life on several worlds other than Earth, even conceivably intelligent life, the chances are not high. Furthermore, the chances would seem to be virtually zero that a technological civilization exists, or could exist, anywhere in the Solar system but on Earth.

Nevertheless, the Solar system is by no means the entire Universe. Let us look elsewhere.

We might imagine life in open space in the form of concentrations of energy fields, or as animated clouds of dust and gas, but there is no hint of evidence that such a thing is possible. Until such evidence is forthcoming (and naturally the scientific mind is not closed to the possibility), we must assume that life is to be found only in association with solid worlds at temperatures less than those of the stars.

The only cool, solid worlds we know are the planetary and subplanetary bodies that circle our Sun, but we cannot assume from this that all such bodies in the Universe must be associated with stars.*

There may be clouds of dust and gas of considerably smaller mass than that from which our Solar system originated, and these may have ended by condensing into bodies much smaller than the Sun. If the bodies are sufficiently smaller than the Sun, say with only 1/50 the mass or less, they would end by being insufficiently massive to ignite into nuclear fire. The surfaces of such bodies would remain cool and they would resemble planets in their properties, except that they would follow independent motions through space and would not be circling a star.

All our experience teaches us that of any given type of astronomical body, the number increases as the size decreases. There are a greater number of small stars than of large ones, a greater number of small planets than large ones, a greater number of small satellites than large ones, and so on. Might we argue from that, that these substars, too small to ignite, are far greater in number than those similar bodies that are massive enough to ignite? At least one important astronomer, the American Harlow Shapley (1885–1972), has very strongly advanced the likelihood of the existence of such bodies.

Naturally, since they do not shine, they remain undetected and we are unaware of them. But if they exist, we might reason that there exist substars in space through an entire range of sizes from super-Jupiters to small asteroids. We might even suppose that the larger ones could have bodies considerably smaller than themselves circling them, much as there are bodies circling Jupiter and the other giant planets within our own Solar system.

The question is, though: Would life form on such substars?

So far I have suggested that the irreducible requirements for life (as we know it) are, first, a free liquid, preferably water, and, second, organic compounds. A third requirement, which ordinarily we take for granted, must be added, and that is energy. The energy is needed to build the organic compounds out of the small molecules present at the start, small molecules such as water, ammonia, and methane.

Where would the energy come from in these substars?

---

* Our Sun, it is perhaps needless to say, is a star, and seems so different from all the rest only because it is so much closer to us.

In the condensation of a cloud of dust and gas into a body of any size, the inward motion of the components of the cloud represents kinetic energy obtained from the gravitational field. When the motion stops, with collision and coalescences, the kinetic energy is turned into heat. The center of every sizable body is therefore hot. The temperature at the center of the Earth, for instance, is estimated to be 5,000° C (9,000° F).

The larger the body and the more intense the gravitational field that formed it, the greater the kinetic energy, the greater the heat, and the higher the internal temperature. The temperature at the center of Jupiter, for instance, is estimated to be 54,000° C (100,000° F).

It might be expected that this internal heat is a temporary phenomenon and that a planet would slowly but surely cool down. So it would, if there were no internal supply of energy to replace the heat as it leaked away into space.

In the case of Earth, for instance, the internal heat leaks away very slowly indeed, thanks to the excellent insulating effect of the outer layers of rock. At the same time, those outer layers contain small quantities of radioactive elements such as uranium and thorium, which, in their radioactive breakdown, liberate heat in large enough quantities to replace that which is lost. As a result, the Earth is not cooling off perceptibly, and though it has existed as a solid body for 4,600,000,000 years, its internal heat is still there.

In the case of Jupiter, there seem to be some nuclear reactions going on in the center, some faint sparks of starlike behavior, so that Jupiter actually radiates into space three times as much heat as it receives from the Sun.

This long-lasting internal heat would be more than ample to support life, if living things could tap it.

We could fantasize life as existing within the body of a planet where nearby pockets of heat might have served as the energy source to form and maintain it. There is, however, no evidence that life can exist anywhere but at or near the surface of a world, and until evidence to the contrary is obtained, we should consider surfaces only.

Suppose, then, we consider a substar no more massive than the Earth; or a body that massive that is circling a substar somewhat more massive than Jupiter but yielding no visible light.

Such an Earthlike body, whether free in space or circling a substar, would tend to be a world like Ganymede or Callisto. There would be internal heat, but, thanks to the insulating effect of the outer layers, very little would leak outward to the surface; any more than Earth's internal heat leaks outward to melt the snow of the polar regions and mitigate the frigidity of Earth's temperatures.

To be sure, on Earth there are local leaks of considerable magnitude, producing hot springs, geysers, and even volcanoes. We might imagine such things on Earth-sized substars as well. In addition, there could be energy derived from the lightning of thunderstorms. Still, whether such sporadic energy sources would meet the requirements for forming and maintaining life is questionable. There is also the point that a world without a major source of light from a nearby star may be unfit for the development of intelligence—a subject I will take up later in the book.

The Earth-sized substar would be composed of a much larger percentage of volatiles than Earth itself, since there would have been no nearby hot star to raise the temperature in surrounding space and make the collection of volatiles impossible. Therefore, again as on Ganymede and Callisto, we might imagine a world-girdling ocean, probably of water, kept liquid by internal heat, but covered by a thick crust of ice.

Substars still smaller than the Earth would have less internal heat and would be even more likely to be icy, have less in the way of sporadic sources of appreciable energy, have smaller internal oceans or none at all.

If a body were small enough to attract little or no volatile matter even at the low temperatures that would exist in the absence of a nearby star, it would be an asteroidal body of rock or metal or both.

What about substars that are larger than Earth and therefore possess greater and more intense reservoirs of internal heat? Such a larger body is bound to be Jupiterlike. A large substar is certain to be made up largely of volatile matter, particularly hydrogen and helium; and high internal heat will make the planet entirely liquid.

Heat can circulate much more freely through liquid by convection than through solids by slow conduction. We can expect ample heat at or near the surface in such large substars and the heat may remain ample for billions of years. However, again the most we can expect on a large substar is intelligent life of the dolphin variety—and no technological civilization.

In short, the formation of substars would rather resemble the formation of bodies in the outer Solar system, and we may expect no more of the former than of the latter.

For a technological civilization, we need a solid planet with both oceans and dry land, so that life as we know it can develop in the former and emerge on the latter. To form such a world there must be a nearby star to supply the heat that would drive away most of the volatile matter, but not all. The nearby star would also supply the necessary energy for the formation and maintenance of life in a copious and steady manner.

In that case, we must concentrate our attention on the stars. These, at least, we can see. We know they exist and need not simply assume the probability of their existence as in the case of the substars.

THE MILKY WAY

If we turn to the stars and consider them as energy sources in the neighborhood of which we may find life, possibly intelligence, and possibly even technological civilizations, our first impression may be heartening, for there seem to be a great many of them. Therefore, if we fail to find life in connection with one, we may do so in connection with another.

In fact, the stars may well have impressed the early, less sophisticated watchers of the sky as innumerable. Thus, according to the Biblical story, when the Lord wished to assure the patriarch Abraham that, despite his childlessness, he would be the ancestor of many people, this is how it is described:

"And he [God] brought him [Abraham] forth abroad, and said, 'Look now toward heaven, and tell the stars, if thou be able to number them'; and he [God] said unto him [Abraham], 'So shall thy seed be.'"

Yet if God were promising Abraham that he would ultimately have as many descendants as there were stars in the sky that he could see, God was not promising as much as might be assumed.

The stars have been counted by later generations of astronomers who were less impressed with their innumerability. It turns out the number of stars that can be seen with the unaided eye (assuming excellent vision) is, in total, about 6,000.

At any one time, of course, half the stars are below the horizon, and others, while present above the horizon, are so near it as to be blotted out through light absorption by an unusually great thickness of even clear air. It follows that on a cloudless, moonless night, far from all man-made illumination, even a person with excellent eyes cannot see more than about 2,500 stars at one time.

In the days when philosophers assumed all worlds were inhabited and when general statements to that effect were made, it is not clear whether any particular philosopher truly understood the nature of stars.

Perhaps the first clear statement of the modern view was that of Nicholas of Cusa (1401–1464), a cardinal of the Church, who had particularly striking ideas for his time. He thought that space was infinite and that there was no center to the Universe. He thought all things moved, including the Earth. He also thought the stars were distant Suns, that they were attended by planets as the Sun was, and that those planets were inhabited.

Interesting, but we of the contemporary world are less sanguine concerning habitability, and cannot accept in carefree fashion the notion of life everywhere. We know there are dead worlds, and we know that there are others, which while possibly not dead, are not likely to bear more than simple bacteria life forms of life. Why may there not be stars around which only dead worlds orbit? Or around which no worlds circle at all?

If it should turn out that habitability is associated with only a small percentage of the stars (as life seems to be associated with only a small percentage of the worlds of the Solar system), then it becomes important to determine whether there are stars other than those we happen to be able to see and if so, how many. After all, the greater the number of stars, the greater the chance of numerous life forms existing in space even if the chances for any one star are very low.

The natural assumption, of course, is that only those stars exist that can be seen. To be sure, some stars are so dim that excellent eyes can just barely make them out. Might it not seem natural to suppose that there are some that are fainter still and cannot be made out by even the best eyes?

Apparently, this seemed to occur to very few. Perhaps there was the unspoken feeling that God wouldn't create something too dim to be seen, since what purpose could such an object serve? To suppose that everything in the sky was there only because it affected human beings (the basis of astrological beliefs) seemed to argue against invisible bodies.

The English mathematician Thomas Digges (1543–1595) did espouse views like those of Nicholas of Cusa and in 1575 maintained not only infinite space, but an infinite number of stars spread evenly throughout it. Italian philosopher Giordano Bruno (1548–1600) also argued the same views, and did so in so undiplomatic and contentious a manner that he was finally burned at the stake in Rome for his heresies.

The argument over the matter ended in 1609, however, thanks to Galileo and his telescope. When Galileo turned his telescope on the sky, he immediately discovered that he saw more stars with his instrument than without it. Wherever he looked, he saw stars that could not be seen otherwise.

Without a telescope one saw six stars in the tiny little star group called the Pleiades. There were legends of a seventh that had dimmed and grown invisible. Galileo not only saw this seventh star easily once he clapped his telescope to his eyes, he saw thirty more stars in addition.

Even more important was what happened when he looked through his telescope at the Milky Way.

The Milky Way is a faint, luminous fog that seems to form a belt around the sky. In some ancient myths, it was pictured as a bridge connecting heaven and Earth. To the Greeks it was sometimes seen as a spray of milk from the divine breast of the goddess Hera. A more materialistic way of looking at the Milky Way, prior to the invention of the telescope, was to suppose it was a belt of unformed star matter.

When Galileo looked at the Milky Way, however, he saw it was made up of myriads of very faint stars. For the first time, a true notion of how numerous the stars actually were broke in on the consciousness of human beings. If God had granted Abraham telescopic vision, the assurance of innumerable descendants would have been formidable indeed.

The Milky Way, by its very existence, ran counter to Digges' view of an infinite number of stars spread evenly through infinite

System of Stars Shaped Like a Coin

Few
stars
visible

Many
stars
visible

The Milky Way

space. If that were so, then the telescope should reveal roughly equal numbers of stars in whatever direction it was pointed. As it was, it was clear that the stars did not stretch out equally in all directions, but that they made up a conglomerate with a definite shape to it.

The first to maintain this was the British scientist Thomas Wright (1711–1786). In 1750, he suggested that the system of stars might be shaped rather like a coin, with the Solar system near its center. If we looked out toward the flat edges on either side, we saw relatively few stars before reaching the edge, beyond which there was none. If, on the other hand, we looked out along the long axis of the coin in any direction, the edge was so distant that the very numerous, very distant stars melted together into dim milkiness.

The Milky Way, therefore, was the result of the vision following the long axis of the stellar system. In all other directions, the edge of the stellar system was comparatively nearby.

The whole stellar system can be called the Milky Way, but one usually goes back to the Greek phrase for it, which is *galaxias kyklos (milky circle)*. We call the stellar system the Galaxy.

THE GALAXY

The shape of the Galaxy could be determined more accurately if one could count the number of stars visible in different parts of the sky, and then work out the shape that would yield those numbers. In 1784, William Herschel undertook the task.

To count all the stars all over the sky was, of course, an impractical undertaking, but Herschel realized it would be quite proper to be satisfied with sampling the sky. He chose 683 regions, well scattered over the sky, and counted the stars visible in his telescope in each one. He found that the number of stars per unit area of sky rose steadily as one approached the Milky Way, was maximal in the plane of the Milky Way, and minimal in the direction at right angles to that plane.

From the number of stars he could see in the various directions, Herschel even felt justified in making a rough estimate of the total number of stars in the Galaxy. He decided that it contained 300 million stars, or 50,000 times as many as could be seen with the unaided eye. What's more, he decided that the Galaxy was five times as long in its long diameter as in its short.

He suggested that the long diameter of the Galaxy was 800 times the distance between the Sun and the bright star Sirius. At the time, the distance was not known, but we now know it to be 8.63 light-years, where a light-year is the distance light will travel in one year.*

Herschel's estimate, therefore was that the Galaxy was shaped like a grindstone, and was about 7,000 light-years across its long diameter and 1,300 light-years across its short diameter. Since the Milky Way seemed more or less equally bright in all directions, the Sun was taken to be at or near the center of the Galaxy.

More than a century later, the task was undertaken again by the Dutch astronomer Jacobus Cornelius Kapteyn (1851–1922). He had the technique of photography at his disposal, which made things a bit easier for him. He, too, ended with the decision that the Galaxy was grindstone-shaped with the Sun near its center. His estimate of the size of the Galaxy was greater than Herschel's, however.

In 1906, he estimated the long diameter of the Galaxy to be 23,000 light-years and the short diameter to be 6,000 light-years. By 1920, he had further raised the dimensions to 55,000 and 11,000 respectively. The final set of dimensions involved a Galaxy with a

---

* Since light travels at the rate of 299,792 kilometers (186,282 miles) per second, a light-year is 9,460,000,000,000 kilometers (5,878,500,000,000 miles) long. The distance of Sirius is therefore 82 trillion kilometers (50 trillion miles). It is simpler to use light-years.

volume 520 times that of Herschel's.

Even as Kapteyn was completing this survey of the Galaxy, a totally new outlook had entered astronomical thinking.

It came to be recognized that the Milky Way was full of clouds of dust and gas (like the one that had served as the origin of our Solar system and, perhaps, of others) and that those clouds blocked vision. Thanks to those clouds, we could only see our own neighborhood of the Galaxy and in that neighborhood we were at the center. Beyond the clouds, though, there might well be vast regions of stars we could not see.

Indeed, as new methods for estimating the distance of far-off star clusters were developed, it turned out that the Sun was not in or near the center of the Galaxy at all, but was far off in the outskirts. The first to demonstrate this was Harlow Shapley, who in 1918 presented evidence leading to the belief that the center of the Galaxy was a long distance away in the direction of the constellation Sagittarius, where, as it happens, the Milky Way is particularly thick and luminous. The actual center was, however, hidden by dust clouds, as were the regions on the other side of the center.

Through the 1920s, Shapley's suggestion was investigated and confirmed, and by 1930 the dimensions of the Galaxy were finally worked out, thanks to the labors of the Swiss-American astronomer Robert Julius Trumpler (1886–1956).

The Galaxy is more nearly lens shaped than grindstone shaped. That is, it is thickest at the center and grows thinner toward its edges. It is 100,000 light-years across and the Sun is about 27,000 light-years from the center, or roughly halfway from the center toward one edge.

The thickness of the Galaxy is about 16,000 light-years at the center and about 3,000 light-years at the position of the Sun. The Sun is located about halfway between the upper and lower edge of the Galaxy, which is why the Milky Way seems to cut the sky into two equal halves.

The Galaxy, as it is now known to be, is four times the volume of Kapteyn's largest estimate.

In a way, the Galaxy resembles an enormous Solar system. In the center, playing the part of the Sun, is a spherical "Galactic nucleus" with a diameter of 16,000 light-years. This makes up only a small portion of the total volume of the Galaxy, but it contains most of the

Suppose we consider two patches of luminosity in the sky that look like isolated regions of the Milky Way, and that are so far south in the sky as to be invisible to viewers in the North Temperate Zone. They were first described in 1521 by the chronicler accompanying Magellan's voyage of circumnavigation of the globe—so they are called the Large Magellanic Cloud and the Small Magellanic Cloud.

They were not studied in detail until John Herschel observed them from the astronomic observatory at the Cape of Good Hope in 1834 (the expedition that fueled the Moon Hoax). Like the Milky Way, the Magellanic Clouds turned out to be assemblages of vast numbers of very dim stars, dim because of their distance.

In the first decade of the twentieth century, the American astronomer Henrietta Swan Leavitt (1868–1921) studied certain variable stars in the Magellanic Clouds. By 1912, the use of these variable stars (called Cepheid variables because the first to be discovered was in the constellation Cepheus) made it possible to measure vast distances that could not be estimated in other ways.

The Large Magellanic Cloud turned out to be 170,000 light-years away and the Small Magellanic Cloud 200,000 light-years away. Both are well outside the Galaxy. Each is a galaxy in its own right.

They are not large, however. The Large Magellanic Cloud may include perhaps 10 billion stars and the Small Magellanic Cloud only about 2 billion. Our Galaxy (which we may refer to as the Milky Way Galaxy if we wish to distinguish it from others) is 25 times as large as both Magellanic Clouds put together. We might consider the Magellanic Clouds as satellite galaxies of the Milky Way Galaxy.

Is this all, then?

A certain suspicion arose concerning a faint, fuzzy patch of cloudy matter in the constellation Andromeda; a patch of dim light called the Andromeda Nebula. Even the best telescopes could not make it separate into a conglomeration of dim stars. A natural conclusion was, therefore, that it was a glowing cloud of dust and gas.

Such glowing clouds were indeed known, but they did not glow of themselves. They glowed because there were stars within them. No visible stars could be seen within the Andromeda Nebula. The light from other luminous clouds when analyzed, however, turned out to be completely different from starlight; whereas the light of the Andromeda Nebula was exactly like starlight.

Another alternative, then, was that the Andromeda Nebula was a conglomeration of stars, but one that was even more distant than the Magellanic Clouds, so that the individual stars could not be made out.

When Thomas Wright had first suggested in 1750 that the visible stars were collected into a flat disc, he theorized that there might be other such flat discs of stars at great distances from our own. This idea was taken up by the German philosopher Immanuel Kant (1724–1804) in 1755. Kant spoke of "island universes."

The notion did not catch on. Indeed, when Laplace developed his notion that the Solar system had formed out of a whirling cloud of dust and gas, he cited the Andromeda Nebula as an example of a cloud slowly whirling and contracting to form a sun and its attendant planets. That was the reason the theory was called the nebular hypothesis.

By the time the twentieth century opened, however, the old notion of Wright and Kant was gathering strength. Occasionally, stars did appear in the Andromeda Nebula, stars that were clearly "novas"; that is, stars that suddenly brightened several magnitudes and then dimmed again. It was as though there were stars in the Andromeda Nebula that were ordinarily too dim to see under any circumstances because of their great distances, but that, upon briefly brightening with explosive violence, became just bright enough to make out.

There are such novas, now and then, among the stars of our own Galaxy, and by comparing their apparent brightness with the brightness of the very dim novas in the Andromeda Nebula, the distance of the Andromeda could be roughly worked out.

By 1917, the argument was settled. A new telescope with a 100-inch mirror had been installed on Mt. Wilson, just northeast of Pasadena, California. It was the largest and best telescope that existed up to that time. The American astronomer Edwin Powell Hubble (1889–1953), using that telescope, was finally able to resolve the outskirts of the Andromeda Nebula into masses of very faint stars.

It was the "Andromeda Galaxy" from that point on.

By the best modern methods of distance determination, it would appear that the Andromeda Galaxy is 2,200,000 light-years distant, eleven times as far away as the Magellanic Clouds. No wonder it was difficult to make out the individual stars.

The Andromeda Galaxy is no dwarf, however. It is perhaps twice as large as the Milky Way Galaxy and may contain up to 600 billion stars.

The Milky Way Galaxy, the Andromeda Galaxy, and the two Magellanic Clouds are bound together gravitationally. They form a "galactic cluster" called the Local Group and are not the only members, either. There are some twenty members altogether. There is one, Maffei I, which is about 3,200,000 light-years away, and it is just about as large as the Milky Way. The remainder are all small galaxies, a couple with less than a million stars apiece.

There may be as many as 1.5 trillion stars in the Local Group altogether, but that isn't all there are either.

Beyond the Local Group, there are other galaxies, some single, some in small groups, some in gigantic clusters of thousands. Up to a billion galaxies can be detected by modern telescopes, stretching out to distances of a billion light-years.

Even that is not all there is. There is reason to think that, given good enough instruments, we could make observations as far as 12 billion light-years away before reaching an absolute limit beyond which observation is impossible. It may be that there are 100 billion galaxies, therefore, in the observable universe.

Just as the Sun is a star of intermediate size, the Milky Way Galaxy is one of intermediate size. There are galaxies with masses 100 times larger than that of the Milky Way Galaxy, and tiny galaxies with only a hundred-thousandth the mass of the Milky Way Galaxy.

Again, the small objects of a particular class greatly outnumber the large objects, and we might estimate rather roughly that there are on the average 10 billion stars to a galaxy, so that the average galaxy is of the size of the Large Magellanic Cloud.

That would mean that in the observable universe, there are as many as 1,000,000,000,000,000,000,000 (a billion trillion) stars.

This one consideration alone makes it almost certain extraterrestrial intelligence exists. After all, the existence of intelligence is not a zero-probability matter, since *we* exist. And if it is merely a near-zero probability, considering that near-zero probability for each of a billion trillion stars makes it almost certain that somewhere among them intelligence and even technological civilizations exist.

If, for instance, the probability were only one in a billion that near a given star there existed a technological civilization, that would mean that in the Universe as a whole, a trillion different such civilizations would exist.

Let us move on, though, and see if there is any way we can put actual figures to the estimates; or, at least, the best figures we can.

In doing so, let us concentrate on our own Galaxy. If there are extraterrestrial civilizations in the Universe, those in our own Galaxy are clearly of greatest interest to us since they would be far closer to us than any others. And any figures we arrive at that are of interest in connection with our own Galaxy can always be easily converted into figures of significance for the others.

Begin with a figure that deals with our Galaxy and divide it by 30 and you will have the analogous figure for the average galaxy. Begin with a figure that deals with our Galaxy and multiply it by 3.3 billion and you have the analogous figure for the entire Universe.

We start then with a figure we have already mentioned:

1—*The number of stars in our Galaxy* = 300,000,000,000.

The Swedish astronomer Hannes Olof Gösta Alfven (1908–   ) worked out a detailed description of the manner in which the Sun gave off material in its early days (like the Solar wind of today, but stronger) and how this material, under the influence of the Sun's electromagnetic field, picked up angular momentum. It was the electromagnetic field that transferred angular momentum from the Sun to material outside the Sun and made it possible for the planets to be as far from the Sun as they are and to possess as much angular momentum as they do.

Now, a third of a century from the return of the nebular hypothesis, astronomers accept it with considerable confidence, along with its consequences.

In the new version of the nebular hypothesis, the outer planets are not older than the inner planets; all the planets and the Sun itself are of the same age.

Furthermore, if the Sun and the planets formed out of the same whirlpools of dust and gas, all developing in the same process, then this is very likely the way in which any star like the Sun (and just possibly any star at all) develops. There should, in that case, be very many planetary systems in the Universe and just possibly as many planetary systems as there are stars.

THE ROTATING STARS

Is there any way we can check this suggestion of the universality of planetary systems? Theories are all very well, but if there is any physical evidence that can be gathered, however tenuous, so much the better.

Suppose we had evidence to show that planetary systems were few. We would have to suppose the Weizsäcker theory of star formation was wrong, or at least that it must be seriously modified. Perhaps the Sun formed in lonely splendor, and then passed through another cloud of dust and gas in space (there are plenty of such clouds) and collected some of it gravitationally. In that case, turbulences in the second cloud might finally form the planets, which would be younger than the Sun, perhaps a great deal younger.

This would be a return to a form of catastrophism, even though the passing of the Sun through a cloud of gas is not nearly so violent an event as the collision or near collision of two stars. It is still an accidental event and would necessarily result in relatively few planetary systems.

On the other hand, if it turned out that the evidence clearly indicated that a great many stars happened to have planets, then we could not possibly expect this to happen in any catastrophic way. Some version of the nebular hypothesis with the automatic or near-automatic formation of planets along with a star would have to be correct.

The trouble is, though, that we can't see whether any stars have planets in attendance. Even at the distance of the nearest star (Alpha Centauri, which is 4.3 light-years from us) there would be no way of actually seeing even a large planet the size of Jupiter or greater. Such a planet would be too small to see by the reflected light of its star. Even if a telescope were invented that could make out that dim flicker of reflected light, the nearness of the much greater light of its star would utterly drown it out.

We must give up hope of direct sighting then, at least for now, and resort to indirect means.

Consider our own Sun, which is a star that certainly has a planetary system. The remarkable thing about the Sun is that it rotates so slowly on its axis that 98 percent of the angular momentum of the system resides in the insignificant mass of its planets.

If angular momentum passed from the Sun to its planets when those planets were formed (by any mechanism), then it is reasonable to suppose that angular momentum might pass from any star to its planets. If, then, a star has a planetary system, we would expect it to spin on its axis relatively slowly; if it does not, we would expect it to spin relatively rapidly.

But how does one go about measuring the rate at which a star spins when even in our best telescopes it appears as only a point of light?

Actually, there is much that can be deduced from starlight even if the star itself is but a point of light. Starlight is a mixture of light of all wavelengths. The light can be spread out in order of wavelength from the short waves of violet light to the long waves of red light, and the result is a "spectrum." The instrument by which the spectrum is produced is the "spectroscope."

The spectrum was first demonstrated in the case of sunlight by Isaac Newton in 1665. In 1814, the German physicist Joseph von Fraunhofer (1787–1826) showed that the Solar spectrum was crossed by numerous dark lines, which, it was eventually realized, represented missing wavelengths. They were wavelengths of light that were absorbed by atoms in the Sun's atmosphere before they could reach the Earth.

In 1859, the German physicist Gustav Robert Kirchhoff (1824–1887) showed that the dark lines in the spectrum were "fingerprints" of the various elements, since the atoms of each element emitted or absorbed particular wavelengths that the atoms of no other element emitted or absorbed. Not only could spectroscopy be used to analyze minerals on Earth, but it could be used to analyze the chemical makeup of the Sun.

Meanwhile, the art of spectroscopy had been refined to the point where the light of stars, though much dimmer than the light of the Sun, could also be spread out into spectra.

From the dark lines in the stellar spectra much could be worked out. If, for instance, the dark lines in the spectrum of a particular star were slightly displaced toward the red end, then the star would be receding from us at a speed that could be calculated from the extent of the displacement. If the dark lines were displaced toward the violet end of the spectrum, the star would be approaching us.

The significance of this "red shift" or "violet shift" was quite evident from work that had been done on sound waves in 1842 by the Austrian physicist Christian Johann Doppler (1803–1853) and then applied to light waves in 1848 by the French physicist Armand Hippolyte Louis Fizeau (1819–1896).

Suppose, now, that a star is rotating and that it is so situated in space that neither of its poles is facing us, but that each pole is located at or near the sides of the star as we view it. In that case, at one side of the star between the poles the surface is coming toward us, and on the opposite side it is receding from us. The light from one side causes the dark lines to shift slightly toward the violet, the light from the other causes them to shift slightly toward the red. The dark lines, shifting perforce in both directions, grow wider than normal. The more rapidly the star rotates, the wider the dark lines in the spectrum.

This was first suggested in 1877 by the English astronomer William de Wiveleslie Abney (1843–1920); and the first actual discovery of broad lines produced by rotation came in 1909 through the work of the American astronomer Frank Schlesinger (1871–1943). It was only in the mid-1920s, however, that studies on the rotation of stars began to be common and the Russian-American astronomer Otto Struve (1897–1963) was particularly active here.

It was indeed found that some stars do rotate slowly. A spot on the Sun's equator travels only about 2 kilometers (1¼ miles) per second as the Sun makes its slow rotation on its axis, and many stars rotate with that equatorial speed or not very much more. On the other hand, some stars whirl so rapidly on their axis as to attain equatorial speeds of anywhere from 250 to 500 kilometers (165 to 330 miles) per second.

It is tempting to assume that the slow-rotators have planets and have lost angular momentum to them, while the fast-rotators do not have planets and have retained all, or almost all, their original angular momentum.

That is not all that can be learned in this way, however. When stellar spectra were first studied, it was clear that while some had spectra resembling that of the Sun, others did not. In fact, stellar spectra differed from each other widely and, as early as 1867, Secchi (the astronomer who had anticipated Schiaparelli's discovery of the Martian canals) suggested that the spectra be divided into classes.

This was done, and eventually the various attempts to label the classes ended in the spectra being listed as O, B, A, F, G, K, and M, with O representing the most massive, the hottest, and the most luminous stars known; B was next, A next, and so on down to M, which included the least massive, the coolest, and the dimmest stars. Our Sun is of spectral class G and is thus intermediate in the list.

As stellar spectra were more and more closely studied, each spectral class could be divided into ten subclasses: B0, B1 . . . B9; A0, A1 . . . A9; and so on. Our Sun is of spectral class G2.

The American astronomer Christian Thomas Elvey (1899–   ), working with Struve, found by 1931 that the more massive a star, the more liable it was to be a fast-rotator. The stars of spectral classes O, B, and A, together with the larger F-stars, from F0 to F2, were very likely to be fast-rotators.

The stars of spectral classes F2–F9, G, K, and M were virtually all slow-rotators.

CHAPTER 7
Sunlike Stars

GIANT STARS

The fact that, according to our conclusions in the previous chapter, there is an enormous number of planetary systems in our Galaxy does not, *in itself,* mean that life is rampant.

Different stars may not be equally suitable as incubators of life on their planets and the next step is, therefore, to consider this possibility and to determine (if we can) which stars are suitable, and how many such suitable stars there might be.

If it turns out that the requirements for a suitable star are exceedingly numerous and complex, it may be that virtually no stars are suitable, and all those planetary systems might as well not be there, as least as far as extraterrestrial intelligence is concerned.

Such extreme pessimism is, however, unnecessary, for we begin with two statements, one of which is absolutely certain.

The certain statement is that our Sun is adequate as an incubator of life, so it is therefore possible for a star to be suitable. The second statement, somewhat less than completely certain but so near

111

to certainty that no astronomer doubts the fact, is that the Sun is not a particularly unusual star. If the Sun is suitable, many stars should be.

Let us begin by asking how stars might differ.

The most obvious point of difference, one that was recognized as soon as inquisitive eyes turned upward toward the night sky, is that the stars differ in brightness.

This difference, of course, may be due entirely to differences in distance. If all stars were equally bright when viewed at a given distance (if all, in other words, were of equal "luminosity"), then those that were nearer to us, in actual fact, would be brighter in appearance than those that were farther from us.

Once the distances of the stars were worked out (the first to accomplish the task, in 1838, was Bessel, who six years later discovered Sirius's companion star) it turned out that the apparent brightnesses were not entirely due to different distances. Some stars are intrinsically more luminous than others.

Some stars are more massive than other stars, too, but mass and luminosity go hand in hand. As Eddington showed in the 1920s, a more massive star *had* to be more luminous. A more massive star had a more intense gravitational field and, in order to keep it from collapsing, the temperature at its center had to be higher. A higher central temperature produced a greater flood of energy pouring out of the star in all directions, and its surface was both hotter and more luminous.*

What is more, luminosity goes up more rapidly than mass. If Star A is two times as massive as Star B, then Star A has a greater tendency to collapse in on itself because its gravitational field is greater. To withstand the greater gravitational field of Star A, the center of that star must be much hotter; sufficiently hotter to make Star A ten times as luminous as Star B.

The most massive stars known are some 70 times the mass of the Sun, but they are 6 million times as luminous. On the other hand, a star with only 1/16 the mass of the Sun (65 times the mass of Jupiter) might be just massive enough to glow a dull red heat, and it would only be one-millionth as luminous as the Sun.

---

* A very massive star may radiate so much of its energy in the invisible ultraviolet region that it will seem less luminous (to the human eye) than one might expect it to be.

atmosphere, so that the planet would be airless a
no more habitable than any other part.

As we imagine a larger and larger star, the e
farther and farther from it. A planet within the ec
subjected to a smaller and smaller tidal effect. Even
were large enough, the tidal effect will no longer be
render the planet unfit for life as we know it.

We might estimate that a star should have at least   of
the Sun (which means it would have to be of spectra class M2 at
least) before a planet in its ecosphere would be suitable for life.

Nor is the matter of tidal effect the only problem with midget
stars. The width of an ecosphere depends on how much energy a star
is radiating. A massive, luminous star has an ecosphere far out in
space and one that is very deep; deeper than the entire width of our
Solar system. A midget star has an ecosphere that is close in on itself
and is very shallow. The chance of a planet's happening to form
within so shallow an ecosphere is vanishingly small.

Finally, stars smaller than spectral class M2 are very often "flare
stars." That is, flares of unusually bright and hot gas periodically
burst out on its surface. This happens on all stars, even on our Sun,
for instance. On the Sun, however, such a flare would only add a
small and bearable fraction to the ordinary Solar output of light and
heat. The same flare on a dim midget star would increase its light and
heat output by up to 50 percent. A planet receiving a proper amount
of energy from the midget star would receive far too much under flare
conditions. The star's role as incubator would be carried out in too
irregular a fashion to be compatible with life.

Between tidal effects, shallowness of ecosphere, and periodic
flares, the exclusion of midget stars from further consideration in
connection with extraterrestrial intelligence is triply justified.

JUST RIGHT

If the stars with too much mass to serve as adequate incubators
for life, those more massive than spectral class F2, make up a small
fraction of all the stars, this is not the case for the stars that are less
massive than spectral class M2 and also don't serve as adequate
incubators for life. Midget stars are very common. More than two-

us of the stars in our Galaxy, and presumably in any galaxy, are too small to be suitable for life.

Between spectral classes F2 and M2 are the stars that range in mass from 1.4 times that of the Sun to 0.33 times that of the Sun. At the upper end of this range, the lifetime of the stars is barely enough to give intelligence a fair chance to evolve. At the lower end of this range, a planet barely escapes tidal effects of too serious a nature.

Within the range, though, are the "Sunlike stars," which, all other things being equal, are suitable incubators for life. While these Sunlike stars do not make up a majority of the stars in the sky, they are not really few in number, either. Perhaps 25 percent of all the stars in the Galaxy are sufficiently Sunlike in character to serve as adequate incubators of life.

That gives us our third figure:

3— *The number of planetary systems in our Galaxy that circle Sunlike stars* = 75,000,000,000.

particular influence on the development of life on the planet.

From the standpoint of this book, therefore, let us talk only of binaries.

There is nothing puzzling about the existence of binaries.

When an initial nebula condenses to form a planetary system, one of the planets may, by the chance of the turbulence, attract enough mass to become a star itself. If, in the course of the development of our own Solar system, Jupiter had accumulated perhaps 65 times as much mass as it did, the loss of that mass to the Sun would not have been particularly significant. The Sun would still have very much the appearance it now has, while Jupiter would be a dim "red dwarf" star. The Sun would then be part of a binary system.

It is even quite possible that the original nebula might condense more or less equally about two centers to form stars of roughly equal mass, each smaller than our Sun, as in the case of the 61 Cygni binary system; or each roughly equal in size to our Sun, as in the case of the Alpha Centauri binary system; or each larger than the Sun, as in the Capella binary system.

The two stars might, if they are of different mass, have radically different histories. The more massive star may leave the main sequence, expand to a red giant, and then explode. Its remnants would then condense to a small, dense star, while the less massive companion star remains on the main sequence. Thus, Sirius has as a companion a white dwarf, a small, dense remnant of a star that once exploded. Procyon also has a white dwarf as a companion.

The total number of binaries in the Galaxy (and presumably in the Universe generally) is surprisingly large. Over the nearly two centuries since their discovery, the estimate of their frequency has steadily risen. At the moment, judging from the examples of those stars close enough to ourselves to be examined in detail, it would seem that anywhere from 50 to 70 percent of all stars are members of a binary system. In order to arrive at a particular figure, let us take an average and say that 60 percent of all stars and, therefore, of all Sunlike stars, too, are members of a binary system.

If we assume that any Sunlike star can form a binary with a star of any mass, then, keeping in mind the proportions of stars of various masses, we could venture a reasonable division of the 75 billion Sunlike stars in the Galaxy as follows:

30 billion (40 percent) are single

25 billion (33 percent) form a binary with a midget star

18 billion (24 percent) form binaries with each other

2 billion (3 percent) form a binary with a giant star

Ought we now to eliminate the 45 billion Sunlike stars involved in binary systems as unfit incubators for life?

Certainly, it would seem that we can omit the 2 billion Sunlike stars that form binaries with giant stars. In their case, long before the Sunlike star has reached an age where intelligence might develop on some planet circling it, the companion star would explode as a supernova. The heat and radiation of a nearby supernova is quite likely to destroy any life on the planet that already existed.

What about the remaining 43 billion Sunlike stars forming a part of binaries?

In the first place, can a binary system possess planets at all?

We might argue that if a nebula condenses into two stars, the two will be twice as effective in picking up debris as one would be. Any planetary material that might escape one would be picked up by the other. In the end, therefore, there would be two stars and no planets.

That this is not necessarily so is demonstrated by the star 61 Cygni, the first whose distance from Earth was determined, in 1838, and that is now known to be 11.1 light-years from us.

61 Cygni, as I have said earlier, is a binary star. The two component stars, 61 Cygni A and 61 Cygni B, are separated by 29 seconds of arc as viewed from Earth (a separation about 1/64 the width of the full Moon).

Each of the component stars is smaller than the Sun, but each is large enough to be Sunlike. 61 Cygni A has about 0.6 times the mass of the Sun, and 61 Cygni B about 0.5 times the mass. The former has a diameter of about 950,000 kilometers (600,000 miles) and the latter a diameter of about 900,000 kilometers (560,000 miles). They are separated by an average distance of about 12,400,000,000 kilometers (7,700,000,000 miles), or a little over twice the average distance between the Sun and Pluto, and they circle each other about their center of gravity once in 720 years.

If we imagined the planet Earth circling one of the 61 Cygni stars at the same distance it now circles the Sun, the other 61 Cygni

This sounds like a large number and, of course, it is, but it represents a measure of our conservatism also. This number means that in our Galaxy, only one star out of 460 can boast a habitable planet. What's more, it is a more conservative figure than some astronomers would suggest. Carl Sagan, who is one of the leading investigators of the possibility of extraterrestrial intelligence, suggests there may be as many as one billion habitable planets in the Galaxy.

only 260 are as primitive as we are—an inconsiderable number. All the rest (meaning just about all of them) are more advanced than we are.

In short, what we find ourselves to have been doing is to have worked out not merely the chances of extraterrestrial intelligence but the chances of superhuman extraterrestrial intelligence.

therefore understanding what death by starvation means and how likely it might be at a given time, a quarrel over food is more likely to be violent and of long duration, and to end in serious injury and death. What is more, even if one individual is beaten and driven off without serious injury to himself, and the food is eaten by the victor, the fight may not be over.

The human being is intelligent enough to hold a grudge. The loser, remembering the injury to his own chances of survival, may then strive to kill the winner by trickery, or from ambush, or by rallying friends—if he cannot do it by main force. And the loser may do this not for any direct good it will do him, or for any increase in the chance of his survival, but out of sheer anger at the memory of the harm done him.

It is not likely that any species other than the human being kills for revenge (or to prevent revenge, since dead people tell no tales and plot no ambushes). This is not because human beings are more evil than other animals, but because they are more intelligent than other animals, and can remember long enough and specifically enough to give meaning to the concept of revenge.

Furthermore, to other species there is little else but food, sex, and the security of the young over which to quarrel. In the case of the human being, however, with his intelligent capacity for foreseeing and remembering, almost any object is liable to set off a spasm of competitive acquisitiveness. The loss of some ornament, or the failure to seize one, may set up a grievance that will lead to violence and death.

And, as civilization approaches and is achieved, human beings develop a more and more materialistic culture, one in which the possession of any number of different things is held to be of value. The development of hunting makes stone axes, spears, bows, and arrows valuable. The coming of agriculture gives land a much greater value than ever before. Rising technology multiplies possessions, and almost anything—from herds of animals, to pottery, to bits of metal— can be equated with economic well-being and social status. Human beings will then have reasons without number to attack, defend, maim, and kill.

Furthermore, the advance of technology cannot help but increase the power of the individual human being to commit effective violence. It is not just a matter of choosing to manufacture swords rather than plowshares. To be sure, some products of technology are designed to kill, but almost *any* product can be used to kill if the anger or fear is there. A good heavy pot, ordinarily used for the most peaceful purposes, can be used to crush a skull.

This continues without limit. Human beings now have at their disposal a series of weapons deadlier than they have ever had, and they still strive for a further intensification of deadliness.

We can conclude that it is impossible for any species to be intelligent without coming to understand the meaning of competition, to foresee the dangers of losing out in competition, to develop an indefinite number of material things and immaterial abstractions over which to compete, and to develop weapons of increasing power that will help them compete.

Consequently, when the time comes where the weapons the intelligent species develops are so powerful and destructive that they outstrip the capacity of the species to recover and rebuild—the civilization automatically comes to an end.

Homo sapiens has, it would seem, run the full gamut and now faces a situation whereby a full-scale thermonuclear war could end civilization—perhaps forever.

Even if we avoid a thermonuclear war, the other concomitants of a developing technology that has been allowed to expand without sufficiently intelligent and thoughtful guidance could do us in. An endlessly expanding population combined with dwindling reserves of energy and material resources would inevitably bring about a period of increasing starvation, which might lead to the desperation of thermonuclear war.

The pollution of the environment may diminish the viability of the Earth—by poisoning it with radioactive wastes from our nuclear power plants, or with chemical wastes from our factories and automobiles, or with something as unremarkable as the carbon dioxide from our burning coal and oil (which may induce a runaway greenhouse effect).

Or civilization may just break down in internal violence without the thermonuclear horror, as the constraints of civilization simply fall apart under the strains of increasing populations and the decline in living standards. We see this already in the rising tide of terrorism.

Well, then, suppose that that is how it always is on any world. A civilization arrives, technological advance accelerates until it reaches civilization, in order to get out into space, develops a planetwide political unit, might there not nevertheless be wars among the worlds?

If we want to wax dramatic, we can imagine civilizations killing each other off with devices that explode whole planets or induce stars to leave the main sequence.

Yet that seems wrong to me. Civilizations that had managed to suppress undue violence on their home worlds would have learned the value of peace. Surely they would not forget it lightly, once off their planet.

Besides, it is not likely that the struggle would be so even that, like the fabled Kilkenny cats, the various civilizations would destroy each other until none was left. Those that were more advanced might win out and establish sway over broader and broader sections of the Galaxy. Indeed, the oldest civilizations, intent on imperial growth, might take over scores, hundreds, thousands of habitable planets before those could develop native civilizations, aborting those civilizations forever.

The half-million habitable worlds might all bear civilizations indeed, but all of those civilizations might belong to any of but a dozen different "Galactic nations," so to speak, maintaining an uneasy peace among themselves. Perhaps the oldest or the mightiest might have managed to take over all the worlds—aborting those civilizations not yet begun, destroying or enslaving those that had gotten a late start—and established a "Galactic Empire."

But if that is so, why haven't we been aborted, taken over, enslaved, destroyed? Where are these Galactic Imperial horrors?

Perhaps they are on their way. The Galaxy is so huge that they just haven't got to us yet.

Surely, that is not very likely. The Galaxy was formed 15 million years ago. Really large stars don't shine for very many million years before exploding, so that by the time the Galaxy was a billion years old or so, there must have been a growing number of second-generation Sunlike stars in the outskirts. Add another 4 billion years for civilizations to develop, and it is possible that some of them have been out in space and expanding now for 10 billion years.

The Galaxy is about 315,000 light-years in circumference, so to go from any point to the antipodes, even the long way round at the very rim, in either direction, will be a little over 150,000 light-years.

That means an expanding civilization would have to travel (on the average) just about the distance from the Earth to the Sun every year, no farther than that, in order to make it around the Galaxy in 10 billion years.

That's just one civilization; as others are added, the rate of colonization from a growing number of nuclei grows. Even supposing no very great speeds, every corner of the habitable portions of the Galaxy must have been thoroughly explored—provided there has been the development of a practical method for interstellar voyaging.

Then why haven't they come here?

Can it be they have just overlooked us—somehow missed us in the crowds of stars?

Not very likely. Our Sun is, of course, a Sunlike star, and I doubt if in 10 billion years of looking, a single such star anywhere in the Galaxy would have been overlooked.

Well, then, if interstellar travel is a practical possibility, we must have been visited; and since Earth has not been taken over and settled and our own independent civilization has in no way been interfered with, it cannot have been by Galactic Imperialists.

Civilizations expanding outward may be far more benign. They may, on principle, allow all habitable planets to develop life in their own way. They may, on principle, establish their bases and seek their resources in those planetary systems that lack habitable planets, making use instead of Marslike or Moonlike worlds.

The different civilizations may have formed a Galactic Federation and our planetary system may be a ward of the Federation, so to speak, until such time as a native civilization appears and advances to the point where it qualifies for membership.

Starships may have us under observation, for all we know. The Austrian-born astronomer Thomas Gold (1920–   ) has suggested, probably in jest, that the first observation vessels may have landed on Earth when it was a new and still sterile planet, and that from the bacterial content of the garbage or wastes left behind, life on Earth began. This is a kind of reincarnation of Arrhenius's suggestion of the seeding of Earth from extraterrestrial spores.

Is all this possible? Could we imagine civilizations so concerned with other civilizations, and not "taking over"?

Perhaps we might reason that half a million civilizations would approach the Universe in half a million different ways, produce half a million sets of cultures, half a million lines of scientific developments, half a million bodies of arts and literatures and amusements and varieties of communications and understandings. Some of all these may be capable of transmission and reception across the gap between intelligent species and, however small the portion so transmitted and received, each species is the better and wiser for it. In fact, such cross-fertilization may increase the life expectancy of each civilization that participates.

VISITS

And if extraterrestrial civilizations have visited Earth and have, on principle, left us to develop freely and undisturbed, might they have visited Earth so recently that human beings had come into existence and were aware of them?

All cultures, after all, have tales of beings with supernormal powers who created and guided human beings in primitive days and who taught them various aspects of technology. Can such tales of gods have arisen from the dim memory of visits of extraterrestrials to Earth in ages not too long past? Instead of life having been seeded on the planet from outer space, could technology have been planted here? Might the extraterrestrials not merely have allowed civilization to develop here, but actually helped it?*

It is an intriguing thought, but there is no evidence in its favor that is in the least convincing.

Certainly, human beings need no visitors from outer space in order to be inspired to create legends. Elaborate legends with only the dimmest kernels of truth have been based on such people as Alexander the Great and Charlemagne, who were completely human actors in the historical drama.

For that matter, even a fictional character such as Sherlock Holmes has been invested with life and reality by millions over the world, and an endless flood of tales is still invented concerning him.

Secondly, the thought that any form of technology sprang up suddenly in human history, or that any artifact was too complex for the humans of the time, so that the intervention of a more sophisti-

---

* This was the central motif of the science fiction movie *2001: A Space Odyssey.*

cated culture must be assumed is about as surely wrong as anything can be.

This dramatic supposition has received its most recent reincarnation in the books of Eric von Däniken. He finds all sorts of ancient works either too enormous (like the pyramids of Egypt) or too mysterious (like markings in the sands of Peru) to be of human manufacture.

Archeologists, however, are quite convinced that even the pyramids could be built with not more than the techniques available in 2500 B.C., plus human ingenuity and muscle. It is a mistake to believe that the ancients were not every bit as intelligent as we. Their technology was more primitive, but their brains were not.

Then, too, all that von Däniken finds mysterious and therefore suggestive of extraterrestrial influence archeologists are convinced they can explain, much more convincingly, in a thoroughly earthly manner.

The conclusion, therefore, is that while there is nothing inconceivable about visits to Earth by extraterrestrial civilizations in the past, even in the near past, there is no acceptable evidence that it has happened, and the evidence deduced for the purpose by various enthusiasts is, as far as we can tell, utterly worthless.

Yet even the visits of ancient astronauts are not the most dramatic suggestions of the sort. There are endless reports of Earth being visited by extraterrestrial civilizations *now*.

Such reports are usually based on the sighting of something that the sighters cannot explain and that they (or someone else on their behalf) explain as representing an interstellar spaceship—often by saying "But what else can it be?" as though their own ignorance is a decisive factor.

As long as human beings have existed, they have experienced things they could not explain. The more sophisticated a human being is, the more widely experienced, the more likely he or she is to expect the inexplicable and to greet it as an interesting challenge to be investigated soberly, if possible, and without jumping to conclusions. The rule is to seek the simplest and most ordinary explanation consistent with the facts and to allow one's self to be driven (with greater and greater reluctance) to the more complex and unusual when nothing less will do. And if one is left with no likely explanation at all, then it must be left there; the sophisticated observer has usually learned to live with uncertainty.

Unsophisticated human beings with limited experience are impatient with puzzles and seek solutions, often pouncing on something they have vaguely heard of if it satisfies an apparently fundamental human need for drama and excitement.

Thus, mysterious lights or sounds, experienced by people living in a society in which angels and demons are commonplace beliefs, will invariably be interpreted as representing angels and demons—or spirits of the dead, or whatever.

In the nineteenth century, they were described as airships on occasion. In the days after World War II, when talk of rocketry reached the general public, they became spaceships.

Thus began the modern craze of "flying saucers" (from an early description in 1947) or, more soberly, "unidentified flying objects," usually abbreviated as UFOs.

That there are such things as unidentified flying objects is beyond dispute. Someone who sees airplane lights and has never seen airplane lights before has seen a UFO. Someone who sees the planet Venus, with its image distorted near the horizon or by a mist, and mistakes it for something much closer, has seen a UFO.

There are thousands of reports of UFOs each year. Many of them are hoaxes; many of them are honest, but capable of a prosaic explanation. A very few of them are honest and entirely mysterious. What of these?

The honestly mysterious sightings are mysterious usually only in that information is insufficient. How much information can someone gather who sees something he cannot understand and sees it without warning and briefly—and grows excited or frightened in the process?

Enthusiasts, of course, consider these mysterious sightings to be evidence of extraterrestrial spaceships. They also consider sightings that are by no means mysterious, but are clear mistakes or even hoaxes, to be evidence of extraterrestrial spaceships. Some of them even report having been on board extraterrestrial spaceships.

There is, however, no reason so far to suppose that any UFO report can represent an extraterrestrial spaceship. An extraterrestrial spaceship is not inconceivable, to be sure, and one may show up tomorrow and will then have to be accepted. But at present there is no acceptable evidence for one.

Those UFO reports that seem to be most honest and reliable

report only mysterious lights. As the reports grow more dramatic, they also grow more unreliable, and all accounts of actual "encounters of the second or third kind" would seem utterly worthless.

Any extraterrestrials reported are always described as essentially human in form, which is so unlikely a possibility that we can dismiss it out of hand. Descriptions of the ship itself and of the scientific devices of the aliens usually betray a great knowledge of science fiction movies of the more primitive kind and no knowledge whatever of real science.

In short, then, once we allow the practicality of easy interstellar travel, we are forced to speculate that Earth is being visited or has been visited, is being helped or at least left alone by a Federation of benevolent civilizations.

Well, perhaps, but none of it sounds compelling. It seems safer to assume that interstellar travel is not easy or practical.

The final conclusion I can come to at the end of the reasoning in this chapter, then, is that extraterrestrial civilizations *do* exist, probably in great numbers, but that we have *not* been visited by them, very likely because interstellar distances are too great to be penetrated.

declining supplies of petroleum and the difficulty of finding a source of energy large enough, safe enough, and long lasting enough to replace it.

The direct use of sunlight would seem to be one possible solution and that sunlight can be gathered more efficiently in space than on Earth's surface. A solar power station can receive the full range of the Sun's energy, unblocked by atmospheric phenomena. If the station is in Earth's equatorial plane in synchronous orbit, at a height of a little over 35,000 kilometers (22,000 miles), it will be in the Earth's shadow only 2 percent of the time over the course of a year.

A number of solar power stations girdling the Earth could solve humanity's energy needs for the indefinite future and could also give Earth's nations a positive reason to cooperate, since building and maintaining the stations would serve as literal lifesavers for each of them alike.

If such solar power stations are understood to be needed and if the effort is made to build them, the space settlements will naturally come into being to house the workers who will serve on the mining stations on the Moon and at the construction sites themselves.

Indeed, beginning with the drive for power stations, space may be put to greater and greater use as observatories, laboratories, and whole factories (much more computerized and automated than they are on the Earth's surface) are lifted into orbit.

With so much of man's industrial and technological activity lifted into space, Earth may return to a more desirable wilderness/park/farm condition. We could restore the beauty of the Earth without losing the material advantages of industry and high technology.

Once the space settlements are established over the next couple of generations as part of a program for meeting the dire need of Earth's population for energy, there may be a number of ancillary advantages.

As the space settlements increase in number, the room available for human beings would increase, too. Within a century, there could conceivably be room for a billion people on space settlements, and within 2 centuries there would be more people in space than on Earth.

This prospect does not obviate the need to lower our birthrate in the long run, for if human beings continue to multiply at their present rate, the total mass of flesh and blood will equal the total mass of the Universe in 9,000 years or so.

In fact, it does not obviate the need to lower our birthrate right now, for long before we could put that first billion into space, Earth's population would have increased by 25 billion and that would be disastrous. And yet the presence of space settlements would offer a bit of an escape valve; the birthrate need not drop quite as far with space settlements in existence.

In addition to allowing some space for human numbers, the burgeoning clusters of space settlements will lend additional variety to human cultures. Each settlement might well have its own way of life, and some might be quite a distance off the norm. Each settlement might have its own styles in clothing, music, art, literature, sex, family life, religion, and so on. The options for creativity in general, and for scientific advance in particular, would be unbounded.

There could even be items of life-style unique to the settlements and impossible to duplicate on Earth.

Mountain climbing on the larger settlements would have comforts and pleasures unknown on Earth. As climbers moved higher, the dowanrd pull of the centrifugal effect induced by the settlement's spin would weaken, and it would be easier to climb still farther. Then, too, the air would grow neither thinner nor colder to any substantial degree.

Finally, in carefully enclosed areas on the mountain tops, where the centrifugal effect is particularly low, people could fly by their own muscle power when they were outfitted with plastic wings on light frames, thanks to the thick air and the small downward pull.

SPACE MARINERS

For the purposes of this book, however, the chief value of the space settlements would be this: They would make possible the exploration of the Solar system—not so much for physical reasons, as for psychological ones.

Consider:

To begin with, space flight is an exotic matter to the people of Earth, something that would take them away from the world on which they live, and on which ancestral life has developed over a stage, and it will be the asteroid belt that will be considered the true home of the settlements. They will be farther from Earth and utterly independent of it, but they can remain within radio and television reach of it, of course. There will be endless room out there for the construction of many millions of settlements without crowding.

The outward push might continue even farther and belts of settlements might be placed around Jupiter and Saturn at distances large enough to avoid the magnetic fields and the charged particles with which those are filled.

In short, the space settlers will prove the Phoenicians, the Vikings, and the Polynesians of the Space Age, venturing out on a far vaster sea to settle their new lands and islands.

By the twenty-third century, the Solar system may well have been thoroughly explored by human beings with settlements in favored places throughout. The Sun itself can serve as an adequate energy source if its radiation is properly gathered and focussed, even far out in the vastness of the outer Solar system, and hydrogen fusion reactors should eventually serve as an alternate adequate source.

STEPPING STONE

This optimistic picture of the total exploration and, so to speak, occupation of the Solar system depends, to a surprising extent, on the use of the Moon as a stepping stone.

Suppose the Moon weren't there in our sky; that it hadn't been formed along with the Earth by some enormously low-probability accident; or that it hadn't been captured late in Earth's life by an equally enormously low-probability accident. Think how that might have affected humanity's technological development.

It was the Moon that first gave human beings the concept of a plurality of worlds. It was the Moon's size and nearness that made it an interesting world and lured us out into space toward what was such a tempting target.

Without the Moon, advancing astronomical techniques might have revealed the planets to be worlds, but would human beings have really tried to develop space travel if the nearest reasonable objects were Venus and Mars, and if flights to the nearest reasonable goal would require a round trip of well over a year?

We need an easy target on which to work out the technology of space flight, and human beings have to be encouraged to strive toward that technology with the bribe of an attainable success.

Of course, human beings might still have sent rockets into space and placed people in orbit around the Earth, even without the presence of the Moon. Such flights have many functions other than that of reaching the Moon. The desire to study Earth as a whole—its resources, its atmosphere and weather pattern, its magnetosphere, the dust and cosmic rays outside the atmosphere, the observation of the rest of the Universe from a position outside the atmosphere, the utilization of solar energy—all would have urged us onward to rocketry and space exploration.

It might all have been less likely without the Moon beckoning us in our fictional dreams, but given the lapse of additional time it might have taken place. Indeed, without the Moon, we could imagine everything that has taken place so far to have taken place anyway, except for the manned and unmanned flights to and past the Moon. Even the probes to the far-distant planets would have taken place.

But would we then have progressed onward to space settlements? If such things seem impractical to many "hardheaded" human beings now, how much more impractical would it seem if all the material for the construction of settlements had to come from Earth itself; if there were no way of using the Moon as a source of raw materials?

And without the space settlements, the true exploration of the Solar system would, in my opinion, be most unlikely.

If, then, it is true that a large Moonlike satellite is a very unlikely possession for an Earthlike habitable planet, and that Earth is the beneficiary of a very rare astronomical accident in this respect, then we must wonder if other civilizations have ever developed space-flight capacity greater than that which we possess right now.

Are other civilizations, one and all, confined to their planet and its immediate environs, and are they capable, at the most, of sending probes to other planets? And is this true, no matter how advanced their technology? It is a tempting thought. It would so neatly explain why the Universe seems so empty, even though half a million and more civilizations may exist in our own Galaxy alone.

It would also offer a sop to our pride. Thanks to our lucky possession of the Moon, it might be that within the next couple of centuries we will develop space-flight capacities far beyond other far, and until they are detected, it is going to be hard to argue their real existence, since no aspect of their properties seems to affect our Universe and therefore compel our belief even in the absence of physical detection.*

Secondly, even if tachyons exist, we have no idea at all of how to turn ordinary particles into tachyons or how to reverse that process. All the difficulties of the photonic drive would be multiplied in the case of the tachyonic drive, for a mistake in simultaneity of conversion would scatter everything not merely over hundreds of thousands of kilometers but perhaps over hundreds of thousands of light-years.

Finally, even if it could all be handled, I still suspect we can't beat the energy requirement; that it would take as much energy to shift matter from one end of the Galaxy to the other by tachyonic drive, as it would by acceleration and deceleration. In fact, the tachyonic drive might take far more energy, since time as well as distance must be defeated.

But we have another possible means of escape. If the qualification "the matter we know" fails us, what about the "Universe we know"? As long as the Universe we worked with was that which Newton knew—the Universe of slow movement and small distances—Newton's laws seemed unassailable.

And as long as the Universe we work with is the one Einstein knew—the Universe of low densities and weak gravitations—Einstein's laws seem unassailable. We might, however, go beyond Einstein's Universe as we have gone beyond Newton's. Consider—

When a large star explodes and collapses, the force of the collapse and the mass of the remnant that is collapsing may combine to drive the subatomic particles together into contact—then smash them and collapse indefinitely toward zero volume and infinite density.

The surface gravity of such a collapsing star builds up to the pitch where anything may fall in but nothing may escape again, so

* For 25 years, physicists accepted the existence of the neutrino even though it had never been detected, because that existence was necessary to explain observed phenomena. Right now, physicists accept the existence of particles called quarks though they have never been detected, because that existence is necessary to explain observed phenomena. There are no observed phenomena that require the existence of tachyons, however, only the manipulation of equations.

that it is like an endlessly deep "hole" in space. Since not even light can escape, it is the "black hole" I mentioned earlier in the book.

Usually one thinks of matter falling into a black hole as being endlessly compressed. There are theories, however, to the effect that if a black hole is rotating (and it is likely that all black holes do), the matter that falls in can squeeze out again somewhere else, like toothpaste blasting out of a fine hole in a stiff tube that is brought under the slow pressure of a steamroller.

The transfer of matter could apparently take place over enormous distances, even millions or billions of light-years, in a trifling period of time. Such transfers can evade the speed-of-light limit because the transfer goes through tunnels or across bridges that do not, strictly speaking, have the time characteristics of our familiar Universe. Indeed, the passageway is sometimes called an Einstein-Rosen bridge because Albert Einstein himself and a coworker named Rosen suggested a theoretical basis for this in the 1930s.

Could black holes someday make interstellar travel or even intergalactic travel possible? By making proper use of black holes, and assuming them to exist in great numbers, one might enter a black hole at point A, emerge at point B (a long distance away) almost at once, and travel through ordinary space to point C, where one enters another black hole and emerges almost at once at point D, and so on. In this way, any point in the Universe might be reached from any other point in a reasonably short time.

Naturally, one would have to work out a very thorough map of the Universe, with black-hole entrances and exits carefully plotted.

We might speculate that once interstellar travel starts in this fashion, those worlds which happen to be near a black-hole entrance would prosper and grow, and space stations would be established still nearer the entrance.

Those space stations can serve as power stations as well, since the energy radiated by matter falling into a black hole can clearly be enormous. We might even visualize space projects that consist of the moving of dead and useless matter into a black hole to increase the energy output (like fueling a furnace).

In fact, this offers still another explanation for the Universe being full of extraterrestrial civilizations that nevertheless do not visit the Earth. It could be that Earth happens to be in a distant backwa-